Spugete

By Joy Cowley

Illustrated by Shane Marsh

Dominie Press, Inc.

Publisher: Christine Yuen
Editor: John S. F. Graham
Designer: Lois Stanfield
Illustrator: Shane Marsh

Published by:

℗ **Dominie Press, Inc.**

1949 Kellogg Avenue
Carlsbad, California 92008 USA

www.dominie.com

Paperback ISBN 0-7685-1084-8
Library Bound Edition ISBN 0-7685-1533-5
Printed in Singapore by PH Productions Pte Ltd
1 2 3 4 5 6 PH 04 03 02

Table of Contents

Chapter One

Know It All

For two years, Tad had been the smartest kid in his class. Then came a new girl with beaded hair and bright eyes who knew all the answers. Her name was Clarene, and although it was her first day, she wasn't at all shy. Tad didn't stand a chance.

Miss Barr had been talking about Abraham Lincoln. She said, "Does anyone know—"

"I do, Miss Barr!" Clarene's hand waved like a flag in a storm.

Miss Barr smiled. "Why, Clarene! I believe

you can read my mind. What was I going to say?"

Clarene replied, "You were going to ask when President Lincoln died, and I was going to tell you 1864."

Miss Barr's smile grew wider. "Well, no, not exactly, Clarene. I was going to ask if anyone knew where I put my whiteboard marker."

Tad knew where Miss Barr's marker was. He raised his hand.

The new girl beat him to it. "It's on your table, Miss Barr, right under your book."

"So it is!" said Miss Barr, picking up the marker. "Thank you, Clarene. I see you are going to be a very helpful student."

"You're welcome, Miss Barr," said Clarene.

"You're welcome, Miss Barr," echoed Tad under his breath.

Miss Barr heard him. She held the marker against the board. "Tad, when was Abraham Lincoln born?"

Tad was good at history. He knew the date, but it had gone clean out of his head.

Miss Barr waited.

Tad cleared his throat.

"1809," said Clarene.

Chapter Two
Spell *Spaghetti*

It was the same with math. The new girl had all the answers. Because Tad was sitting right next to her, he had to put up with her arm waving in his face. It was a real pain.

Miss Barr told them to take out their writing books. "I want you to write about one of your favorite foods, and how it's made."

That was easy for Tad. His father was a chef who did the lunch menu at the Hungry Horse restaurant. At home, Dad made delicious suppers for Tad and his brother Paul.

As Tad wrote, he could almost taste his father's stir-fried chicken. Slices of chicken. Slices of onion and peppers and beans and celery. What else? He chewed his pencil. Some soy sauce. Some ginger. He made a list and then started to describe the cooking part.

"I've finished, Miss Barr," said Clarene.

"Already?" said Miss Barr.

Clarene gave her a big, bright smile and nodded.

"Would you like to read it to the class?" Miss Barr asked.

Tad groaned.

Clarene stood up. "I like Italian food, and my favorite food is spaghetti, but not the sort of spaghetti bought in a can. To make my kind of spaghetti, you need to boil it in water and then you put a sauce on it."

Tad closed his eyes and wished he could close his ears, too. Clarene went on and on, describing the different kinds of sauces she liked. How could anyone write so much in such a short time?

"Good job, Clarene!" said Miss Barr.

As Clarene sat down, Tad leaned over to see her book. This is what he read: *I like talyon food and my favrit food is spugete...*

Tad couldn't help himself. He said in a loud voice, "That's not how you spell *spaghetti*."

Clarene looked at him and then back at her writing.

"Your spelling's all wrong," said Tad. "Look! You've made *bought* into *b-o-t*. *Sauce* is *s-o-u-s*."

Miss Barr came over and stood beside Clarene. After a while, she said, "Don't worry, Clarene. You can fix up the spelling. It's still a good job."

Tad knew that Miss Barr was being nice. He didn't care. He was the best speller in the class, and the new girl was just about the worst.

As Miss Barr walked away, he said to Clarene, "I hope you didn't mind. I was only trying to help."

She turned her big, bright eyes to him. "Go take a long walk on a short pier!" she said.

Chapter Three

The Case of
the Missing Ring

The idea for a detective agency came from Tad's younger brother Paul. "This building needs a couple of good private eyes," he said.

"And I need a new school," replied Tad, who was still upset over Clarene.

"People are always losing things," said Paul. "We'll put a sign in the lobby by the elevator: *Have you lost something? Do you need information? Answer this ad. Hire Paul and Tad.*"

"Tad and Paul," replied Tad.

"That doesn't rhyme," said Paul.

"Well, how about this? *No job too small for Tad and Paul.*"

"My name goes first because it's my agency," said Paul.

"I'm the oldest," Tad said. "I go first or not at all."

Their father came in with a bag of laundry. "What's going on?"

"Tad's in a stinky mood," said Paul.

"Am not!" yelled Tad.

"Cool it, guys!" said Dad. "The way I see it, this is Paul's idea. Tad, you can't be the boss all the time just because you're older."

"What do you mean?" cried Tad. "I don't try to be the boss all the time!"

"Oh, right!" said Dad sarcastically, folding a T-shirt.

Tad's face was hot. "That's not fair!" he cried.

"Okay," said Paul. "We'll put in both rhymes: *Answer this ad. Call Paul and Tad. And No job's too small for Tad and Paul.*"

Their father folded another shirt. "What's your fee?" he said.

"Two dollars for small jobs, and five dollars for big jobs," said Paul.

"Sounds like a good deal," said Dad. "I've got a big job for you. Five days ago, I lost my ring. Sometimes I wear it on my middle finger. But now it's gone." He waved his left hand at them. "I lost it between the apartment and the lobby."

Tad said, "How do you know you didn't lose it at work?"

"Because," said Dad, "I noticed it on my hand when I had breakfast. An hour later,

I was in the lobby. It was a cold day. I was wearing my coat and my brown leather gloves. I took my gloves off to check the mailbox and I noticed the ring was missing."

"Did you take your gloves off in the elevator?" Paul asked.

Dad shook his head as he folded a towel. "No."

"That means," said Tad, "the ring is still in this apartment."

"Our first job's an easy five bucks," Paul said.

"Not that easy," his father replied. "I've already looked for it."

Tad grinned at Paul. It was well known that their father wouldn't find an elephant in his closet unless it stepped on his toes.

"Yep," Tad said. "Piece of cake."

Chapter Four

Sore Loser

The next day, Tad was feeling about as sharp as a wet cornflake. He and Paul had stayed up late, looking for their father's ring. They'd hunted in every drawer. They'd moved all the furniture. Tad had even dug in the herbs growing on the windowsill. No ring.

"It must have gone out in the trash," he told his dad.

"I didn't take out the trash that morning," his dad replied.

"Then where is it?" Tad demanded.

"You're the detectives," said his father. "You tell me."

Paul, who didn't give up easily, said, "We'll look again tonight."

"We've got baseball practice tonight," growled Tad.

"Tomorrow then," said Paul.

Tad didn't feel like baseball practice. He didn't feel like school, either. The spugete girl was terrible, even worse than yesterday. She knew absolutely everything about all the presidents, not just Abraham Lincoln.

During class, Tad leaned toward her. "Bet you can't spell *Constitution*," he muttered.

Miss Barr gave him a sharp look.

But the next time Clarene's hand waved madly in the air, Miss Barr said, "Thank you, Clarene. Maybe now it's someone else's turn to be helpful."

Did that fix her? No, sir! It didn't. That terrible spugete girl went right on waving her hand through the afternoon, until even Miss Barr looked tired.

Tad waited until their teacher was at the back of the class, then he said to Clarene, "Why don't you spell *Declaration of Independence?*"

Clarene scowled at him. "And why don't you spell *sore loser?*" she said.

Chapter Five

Right in Front of Your Nose

Tad and Paul were always hungry after baseball practice.

"Wow!" said Tad. "What's that smell?"

Their dad was in his cooking apron, a spoon in his hand. "Tomatoes," he said. "Basil, garlic, olive oil, and meatballs."

Tad felt his mouth go all juicy. "Cool, man!" he said.

"We're starving!" said Paul.

"That's what I like to hear," said Dad. "Get changed, wash your hands, then set the table. Did you have an okay day?"

"Not bad," said Paul, running for the sink.

"Not good," said Tad.

Dad stirred a pot on the gas burner. "What happened?"

Tad didn't want to talk about it. "Oh, just stuff. I'll survive."

His father nodded. "You need some good news? Your detective agency ad is getting a lot of attention. Dr. Lavalle stopped me in the hall. She said it was a terrific idea. She congratulated me on my brilliant sons."

Tad grinned. Dr. Shawana Lavalle was the new tenant on the floor below. Tad hadn't seen her yet, but he knew she worked at the hospital and was very pretty.

"There's more," said his father. "There are two messages on the answering machine for

your agency. Mrs. Schwartz in 18F wants you to look for her dog's collar. It's black with red stitching. Mr. and Mrs. Ramsay will pay five dollars if you can find a store that sells lemon sherbet candy."

"Really?" Tad said. His rotten, no-good day disappeared. "Two new cases!" he said. "We're in business!"

"I thought you'd be happy," said Dad. "Here, stir this and don't let it burn. Shawana's coming for supper."

"Dr. Lavalle?" Tad ran the spoon around the pot. The sauce bubbled and popped, giving off a wonderful smell.

"That's right." Dad was at the cupboard. "Now, that package of spaghetti! Where did I put it?"

"It's right in front of your nose," said Tad. "Mystery solved. Two dollars, please."

"Very funny," Dad said. He grabbed the package and tore it open. "Her daughter's coming, too. She's about your age. Shawana says spaghetti is her daughter's favorite food."

Tad stopped stirring the sauce. His rotten, no-good day was rushing back, filling him from head to toe. Suddenly, he was no longer hungry.

"What's her daughter's name?" he asked.

"Clarene," said his father.

Chapter Six

Why Didn't I Look There?

Paul was immediately taken with Clarene. He brought out his computer games, his book on dragons, the trophy he got for swimming, and the teddy bear he'd had since he was a baby. That was okay because it meant Tad didn't have to talk to Clarene.

She didn't want to talk to him, either. She'd nearly fallen over with surprise when she saw him. Now she couldn't look at him.

They all sat down to dinner. Dad poured some wine for Dr. Lavalle and himself and then passed the spaghetti around the table. By now, both adults had noticed that Tad and Clarene weren't talking to each other.

Dad gave Tad a long, hard stare. "Pass Clarene the Parmesan cheese," he said.

Tad wanted to say to Clarene, "Spell *Parmesan*," but he didn't dare. He pushed the bowl of cheese along the table. She took it without a word.

Dr. Lavalle looked at Tad's father, and lifted her eyebrows a little. "This is perfect spaghetti," she said. "Isn't it delicious, Clarene?"

Her daughter nodded.

Dr. Lavalle had the same big, bright smile that her daughter had, and she turned it on Tad. "I think your detective agency is fantastic. Where did you get such a great idea?"

Tad mumbled something about Paul.

Their father laughed and said, "These boys are always coming up with something new. If ideas were airplanes, this place would be an airport."

"I'm sure they'll be very successful," said Dr. Lavalle.

Paul sucked up some loose strands of spaghetti. "Nah. We didn't even solve our first case," he said.

Then it all came out, the story of the lost ring.

"We looked everywhere," said Paul.

Clarene sat up, her eyes big and bright. She said, "Did you look in the glove?"

There was a moment of silence. Tad choked on his spaghetti. Why hadn't he looked there?

Dad put down his fork. But before he could get out of his chair, Paul was running to the bedroom. A few seconds later, he came out with the brown leather gloves and handed them to Dad, along with the shining gold ring.

Tad had hoped that it wouldn't be there. He still didn't believe it.

"Well, what do you know?" laughed Dad, rolling the ring around in his fingers. "It must have come off in the glove."

"It couldn't have," said Tad. "You'd have felt it."

"I guess I must have put the gloves in my pocket after I checked the mailbox," his father said. "Yes, I remember now. I was reading the mail, so I didn't put my gloves back on. Well done, Clarene."

Clarene looked pleased with herself.

Paul said, "You're a really good detective, Clarene. I mean really, really good."

Tad was silent. He knew what was going to happen next. He thought it might come from Dr. Lavalle. But it was his father who said it.

"You know something, Clarene? You should join the boys in their detective business."

Chapter Seven

Asking Questions

Dad had made a double-chocolate cheesecake. Tad said he was too tired for dessert. He excused himself and went to bed. He was so mad, he wanted to kick and cry and bite his pillow.

How could this have happened? He had to put up with the terrible spugete girl at school *and* at home. Now she'd invaded their detective agency. She was ruining his life, and he didn't know what to do about it.

After a long time, there was a knock on the door. Paul turned on the light. "You awake, Tad?"

"No!" he snarled.

"Clarene wants to talk to you."

"I don't want to talk to her!" he replied, but it was too late. Clarene was already in the bedroom.

She folded her arms. "You're sulking," she said.

He sat up, "I am not!"

"Yes you are," she said.

"I'm not! I'm not!" he hissed. "Get out of my room!"

Clarene took another step forward. "I'll go when you explain why you don't like me."

That surprised him. He thought for a moment. Then he said, "You think you know everything."

"No I don't," she said.

"Yes you do. You've got all the answers. You don't let anyone else have a say. And

you can't even spell!" He stopped because her eyes had filled with tears.

"I'm sorry," he said. "I didn't mean to say that."

She came farther into the room and rubbed her hand across her eyes. "I don't care what you think. I just came in to tell you I'm not joining your detective agency."

"You're not?"

"I've got better things to do." She put a five-dollar bill next to him on the bed. "You and Paul can have this. Your father gave it to me for finding the ring."

"Keep it," said Tad. "It's yours."

"No," she said. "You guys did all the work. I just asked a question."

Tad scratched the back of his neck. "Yeah, well, asking questions is what the detective business is all about." He tried to smile. "Forget what I said about spelling. Lots of great people couldn't spell."

"I know," she said. "William Shakespeare, Captain Cook, Abraham Lincoln." She folded her arms and sniffed. "I think you hate me because we're alike."

"I didn't say I hated you," he replied.

She went on, "You think *I* know everything because you think *you* know everything." She shrugged. "I guess it means we're both pretty smart."

Tad thought about it. "Could be," he said. He reached across, picked up the five-dollar bill, and put it in his pocket. "You know, you could always be our business consultant."

She looked sideways at him. "What does that involve?"

He said, "If we get stuck on a case, we bring you in on it. You know, we ask your advice."

She nodded. "I guess I could do that."

"Sure, you could," said Tad. "You can start right now, if you like. Case number two and case number three. The mystery of the missing dog collar, and, and—"

"And what?" she asked.

But he was looking at her big, bright smile, and he forgot what he was going to say.